Crystal Meth

Carrie Iorizzo

Crabtree Publishing Company
www.crabtreebooks.com

Developed and produced by:
Plan B Book Packagers
www.planbbookpackagers.com

Editorial director: Ellen Rodger

Art director: Rosie Gowsell-Pattison

Editor: Molly Aloian

Proofreader: Wendy Scavuzzo

Cover design: Margaret Amy Salter

Project coordinator: Kathy Middleton

Production coordinator and
prepress technician: Katherine Berti

Print coordinator: Katherine Berti

Photographs:
Front cover: Slonov/iStockphoto; Title page: Richard Thornton/Shutterstock.com; p. 6: Yuri Arcurs/ Shutterstock.com; p. 8: Andrew Burns/ Shutterstock.com; p. 9: Johan Swanepoel/ Shutterstock.com; p. 11: Stephen Mcsweeny/ Shutterstock.com; p. 12: Sascha Burkard / Shutterstock.com; p. 13: Lack-O'Keen/Shutterstock.com; p. 14: Henk Jacobs/Shutterstock.com; p. 15: Kirill P Shutterstock.com; p. 16: Iakov Kalinin/Shutterstock.com; p. 17: Photo courtesy of Radspunk; p. 18: Anna Hoychuk/ Shutterstock.com; p. 20: Johanna Goodyear/Shutterstock. com; p. 21: (top) Faces of Meth™ photo reproduced with permission from of Multnomah Country Sheriff's Office, (bottom) Photo taken by Dozenist; p. 22: Ampyang/ Shutterstock.com; p. 23: Chris Howey/Shutterstock.com; p. 24: Zurijeta/Shutterstock.com; p. 25: (left) Evgeny Karandaev, (right) Chris Leachman; p. 26: Kiselev Andrey Valerevich/Shutterstock.com; p. 27: Yelbuke/Shutterstock. com; p. 28: Creatista/Shutterstock.com; p. 30: Laurin Rinder/Shutterstock.com; p. 31: Arcady/Shutterstock. com; p. 32: mast3r/Shutterstock.com; p. 33: Malyshev Maksim/Shutterstock.com; p. 34: Piotr Marcinski/ Shutterstock.com; p. 35: Serg Zastavkin/ Shutterstock.com; p. 36: Paul Matthew Photography/Shutterstock.com; p. 37: OtnaYdur/Shutterstock.com; p. 40: ABD/Shutterstock.com; p. 43: Monkey Business Images/Shutterstock.com; p. 44: Phase4Photography/Shutterstock.com; p. 45: Dudarev Mikhail/Shutterstock.com.

Library and Archives Canada Cataloguing in Publication

Iorizzo, Carrie
    Crystal meth / Carrie Iorizzo.

(Dealing with drugs)
Includes index.
Issued also in electronic formats.
ISBN 978-0-7787-5507-4 (bound).--ISBN 978-0-7787-5514-2 (pbk.)

    1. Ice (Drug)--Juvenile literature. 2. Methamphetamine abuse--Juvenile literature. I. Title. II. Series: Dealing with drugs (St. Catharines, Ont.)

HV5822.A5I57 2011   j362.29'95   C2011-907349-8

Library of Congress Cataloging-in-Publication Data

Iorizzo, Carrie.
    Crystal meth / Carrie Iorizzo.
        p. cm. -- (Dealing with drugs)
    Includes index.
    ISBN 978-0-7787-5507-4 (reinforced library binding : alk. paper) -- ISBN 978-0-7787-5514-2 (pbk. : alk. paper) -- ISBN 978-1-4271-8822-9 (electronic pdf) -- ISBN 978-1-4271-9725-2 (electronic html)
    1. Methamphetamine abuse--Juvenile literature. 2. Ice (Drug)--Juvenile literature. I. Title.

RC568.A45I59 2012
616.86'4--dc23

2011044839

Crabtree Publishing Company
www.crabtreebooks.com   1-800-387-7650

Printed in the U.S.A./112011/JA20111018

Published in Canada
Crabtree Publishing
616 Welland Ave.
St. Catharines, Ontario
L2M 5V6

Published in the United States
Crabtree Publishing
PMB 59051
350 Fifth Avenue, 59th Floor
New York, New York 10118

Published in the United Kingdom
Crabtree Publishing
Maritime House
Basin Road North, Hove
BN41 1WR

Published in Australia
Crabtree Publishing
3 Charles Street
Coburg North
VIC 3058

Facts & Stats

An estimated 20 percent of all people who try meth will become hooked. It is extremely addictive and impossible to use recreationally.

Meth is the most widespread and common synthetic drug produced in the United States and is considered rural America's number one illegal drug of choice.

A batch of meth can be made in as little as six hours using common kitchen pots, pans, and other equipment.

Meth labs are very dangerous. Over 15 percent of the meth labs discovered each year are found because of explosion or fire.

Methamphetamine use causes breathing problems, irregular heartbeat, and increased heart rate, which can lead to a stroke and death.

Introduction
Meth Mayhem

What would you do to be the thinnest one in your class, or the only athlete on the team who could finish a marathon run? How far would you go to forget about bad grades at school or troubles at home? What's it like to be on top of the world, even for a day? What if all it took is one pop or rail of a relatively easy-to-find drug called crystal meth. Sounds easy, right? There's an old **adage** that says, if it sounds too good to be true, then it usually is. In the case of meth use, it's not only too good to be true, it's devastating and ultimately deadly.

Crystal meth, or methamphetamine, is an illegal drug that is also called crank or speed on the street. Depending on how it is used, it is known by other names such as ice, crystal, glass, tina, or chalk. Meth produces a **euphoric** high that it is almost immediate. Users feel incredible at first and a high can last several hours. But the "crash" afterward is devastating, and meth is highly addictive. Meth causes side effects that are so serious, they can lead to death. This book will help explain the allure of crystal meth, and why the draw can quickly turn into disaster.

Chapter 1
What's the Big Deal?

Crystal meth is an illegal drug belonging to a group of drugs called amphetamines. Some amphetamines are legally produced and sold as medications. For example, amphetamines are prescribed by doctors for legitimate medical conditions such as a sleep disorder called **narcolepsy**, and a behavioral disorder called Attention Deficit Hyperactivity Disorder (ADHD).

Amphetamines fall under the group of drugs known as narcotics and are monitored by the law in the U.S. under the Controlled Substances Act. They are prescribed only under special medical circumstances, and in low doses, because they are highly addictive and mind-altering. They need to be monitored closely by a doctor. Like all drugs and medications, whether bought over the counter, prescribed by your doctor, or obtained illegally, they change the way you act and the way your body feels and works.

Crystal meth, however, is another story. It is an illegal drug that is made and sold on the street for the sole purpose of getting people high. It does that and more.

Multiple Forms, Multiple Uses

Crystal meth comes in several forms—powder, pill, and crystal—and is used in many ways. The pill or tablets are taken orally. The powder form is snorted through the nose or injected with a needle. It and the crystal form can also be smoked.

Users smoke methamphetamine using a glass pipe or bong. It is often put on aluminum foil and heated and smoked through a tube. Meth is also "hot-railed" by heating one end of a glass pipe and inhaling through the nose at the other, letting the smoke form as it travels up the pipe. It can be dissolved and injected by a needle into a vein, or it can be ground to a fine powder and

snorted. Crystal meth can also be eaten or taken as a "booty bump" by inserting it into the rectum. Sometimes it is mixed with caffeine and made into pills called Kamikaze or yaa baa, which means "crazy medicine." Sometimes meth is mixed with drinks, candies, or drink mixes to hide its bitter flavor.

Crystal meth is sometimes smoked in a glass pipe called an ice pipe.

Instant Rush

Methamphetamine is a more potent version of amphetamines. It affects your **nervous system** on a short-term basis as well as long after the immediate effects have worn off. As soon as you take meth, there is an instant rush that lasts from 5 to 30 minutes, depending on how you take it. This is followed by sensations of alertness, increased activity, decreased appetite, and of being "on the edge."

Crash and Burn

While you are high, your **blood pressure** increases to dangerous levels, your heart rate is elevated and your body temperature can rise as high as 108 degrees F. That is more than high enough to cause a seizure or heart attack. You don't get thirsty, so **dehydration** is common. Even a single dose of methamphetamine can damage the nerves in the center of the brain. When you start to come down, you feel irritable, **agitated**, nervous, and stressed out. You become restless and depressed. You "crash" and may even sleep for up to two days straight.

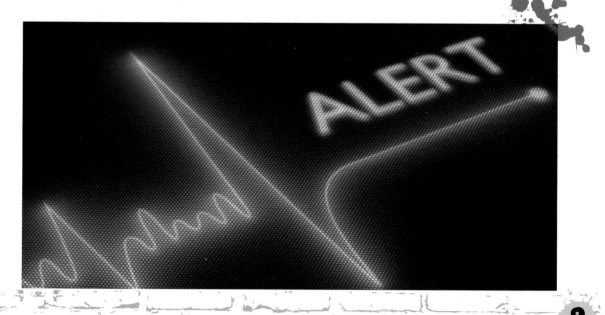

Risky Business

Using methamphetamine is risky business. It is very addictive. You can easily develop a **tolerance** to meth, making it very easy to abuse it. A tolerance means you need higher and higher doses after each use to try to achieve the same high. The agitation and lows are unbearable so, to avoid the crash, users do one hit after the other. This is called bingeing and crashing.

Faster, Higher, Chattier

Methamphetamine gives users a feeling of euphoria, or intense pleasure and happiness. It also makes people feel invincible, as though they can never be overcome, or brought down. Those are pretty intense feelings—but the bad news is, they don't last. Meth addicts are always chasing these feelings, hoping to feel them again and again with each use. The reality is, the euphoria is short-lived and can't be sustained. Users are also often talkative and alert, and can go for days without eating or sleeping. Meth shuts down the area of the brain that controls appetite, so users often lose weight quickly.

Chalk

Street meth is a synthetic, or human-made mixture of chemicals and drugs that is usually mixed, or cut, with baking powder or chalk.

The Law

The Controlled Substances Act of 1970 is the United States' drug policy that regulates the making, possessing, using, and selling of legal and illegal drugs. This law made it illegal to use or possess meth without a prescription. The Methamphetamine Control Act of 1996 increased the penalty for possessing meth and set limits on the amount of meth-related chemicals or materials a person could possess at one time. Some of these materials can be found in drug stores. The Anti-Proliferation Act of 2000 decreased the amount of store-bought meth-making materials, such as some cold medications, that could be bought. The act also brought about programs to educate people about methamphetamine.

Some pharmacies now keep over-the-counter medications containing ephedrine and pseudoephedrine behind the counter to discourage bulk purchases of the drugs that can be used to make meth.

Chapter 2
The Dark Crystal

Methamphetamine is made in illegal labs under dangerous circumstances. It is not the same as the **pharmaceutical** drug that your doctor might prescribe for an illness or medical condition. The sole purpose of making meth is for profit. For the people selling crystal meth, it's a business. It's a way to illegally line their pockets with cash and feed the habits of their customers.

Crystal meth is a chemical cocktail of substances that can be bought at pharmacies, and grocery and department stores. Its recipe is found on hundreds of websites, and it can be made in any kitchen with a frighteningly lethal combination of household ingredients.

Meth Labs in Your Neighborhood

A meth lab does not require fancy equipment. Meth "cooks" don't require a PhD in chemistry to make the drug. "Mom and pop" labs are set up in household kitchens, garages, or barns.

Everyday equipment and appliances such as stoves, pots, and glassware are used. Meth cooks are often careless when cooking their batch of crank. This leads to explosions and fires. For each pound of meth cooked, five or six pounds of toxic waste are produced, and usually left lying around.

Most meth labs have tell-tale signs: windows blacked out so the neighbors and the police can't look in and see what's going on, and a lot of trash strewn about. The trash may include red-tinged coffee filters, fuel cans, duct tape, and chemicals used to make the drug. Meth labs give off a strong, distinctive odor that is a blend of ammonia, ether, drain-cleaner, and other chemicals. Several chemicals are used to make meth. They include lye, anhydrous ammonia, iodine, ether, and over-the-counter cold and sinus medications containing ephedrine and pseudoephedrine.

Meth labs are very dangerous for the people working in them and everyone in the immediate area. When discovered by police, they must be carefully dismantled by crews wearing hazardous materials suits.

Ephedrine and Dopamine

The ephedrine and pseudoephedrine that is put in cold and sinus medications makes your brain release the hormone dopamine. Dopamine is a natural hormone that your brain produces when you eat a big bowl of chocolate ice cream with whipped cream, or laugh until you cry. Dopamine is what makes you feel good.

Unfortunately, crystal meth causes you to eventually lose that "feel good" feeling, making it necessary to do more and more meth to get it back.

Dopamine controls the brain's reward and pleasure centers. Simply put, it makes us happy.

Smells Like Pee

Meth labs often have a strong urine-like smell, due to the combination of chemicals used to make the drug. Labs are flammable, and are often discovered by firefighters responding to fire calls.

So, How Does It Feel?

It feels great! Superman plus, plus! The increased levels of dopamine in your blood make you feel euphoric, unbeatable, supersonic, and indestructible. Your **libido** is heightened and you feel sexually attracted to the opposite sex. You don't feel the need to eat or sleep and you think you can conquer the world.

That's the short term. The long term isn't as pretty. After a few hours, the high starts to wear off. The exhilaration soon turns into extreme nervousness, anxiety, and distress. It feels so awful, you need to take more meth to stop it and bring back the high. And more meth leads to more problems.

The "superhero" effect of meth is tempting, but doesn't last. Over time, users find it impossible to get the same "high." This leads to using larger amounts of the drug.

The Cost of Doing Meth

The cost of meth varies, depending on where you live, how much you buy and the purity of the meth. An ounce of meth (30 grams) costs around $700. A gram (0.1 ounces) costs around $100 and a quarter gram costs about $25.

Supporting a Habit

But the real cost is not in affording it, but in the price your body and mind pay in long-term damage. A $25 hit does not sound expensive. But can you stop at one hit? The answer is an unequivocal "NO"! Meth isn't a recreational drug. It does not take long to develop an addiction. How do you pay for that? How do you keep that under the radar of your family or your friends? Some users lie to their parents about needing money for school trips, books, and clothes. Some steal the money. Other addicts sell the meth and keep enough for personal use. Some users, male and female, sell their bodies for sex to support their habit.

Selling your body for drugs isn't a fair trade. Meth can lead you to make unwise decisions about your safety, including engaging in unsafe sex.

Chapter 3
Meth Head

Crystal meth changes how you see the world, and how the world sees you. Doing meth will change your appearance within a few short months. You will go from a few pimples to zit-city. Your hair will become too greasy to comb. Not that you will care much about it. Don't bother getting braces. Your teeth are going to lose all their **enamel** anyway. These facts might sound outrageous, but they are true. Meth wreaks havoc on your body.

Meth gives "fried" a whole new meaning when describing how your brain looks after doing crystal meth. Not only do you stop looking like you, your brain stops being you. Studies show that meth can do more harm to your brain than coke, alcohol, or heroin. In fact, a study that gave 22 meth users high-intensity **MRI scans** of their brains, found that they lost 11 percent of the limbic part of their brains that controlled their moods, emotions, pleasure, and reward centers. They also lost eight percent of the part of the brain called the hippocampus, which helps you make new memories. This brain tissue wasn't just damaged. The doctor who did the study said, "The (brain) cells are dead and gone." Bye-bye. None left.

Meth "Pretends" to Be Your Friend

Methamphetamine makes your brain swell, causing brain **hemorrhage** or stroke, **paranoia**, and **hallucinations**. It causes your heart to beat abnormally and irregularly which could lead to a heart attack. Meth also mimics the neurotransmitters, or chemical messages, at the brain's dopamine and serotonin receptor sites. In other words, meth pretends to be something it is not, and the brain believes it, so the brain allows the meth to "unlock" the door at the receptor sites. Dopamine and serotonin are then released. Unfortunately, meth then throws away the key and there is no way for dopamine and serotonin to turn off. These hormones are released into the blood stream until the meth wears off. This causes the brain to lose cells that govern the areas that give you pleasure and emotions. Over time, the cells just wear out and die.

Meth affects the areas of your brain that take away your need to eat, sleep, or drink. It causes irritability, confusion, anxiety, dizziness, pupil dilation, tremors, excessive talking, impaired speech, and convulsions.

Pupil dilation is one of the effects of meth use. It's minor compared to the other, more brutal results of using the drug.

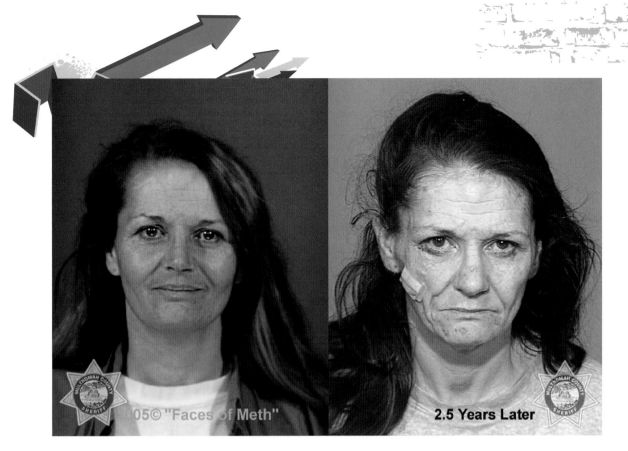

05© "Faces of Meth"   2.5 Years Later

With the permission of meth users, a sheriff's department has released before-and-after photos of meth users as part of an ongoing education program.

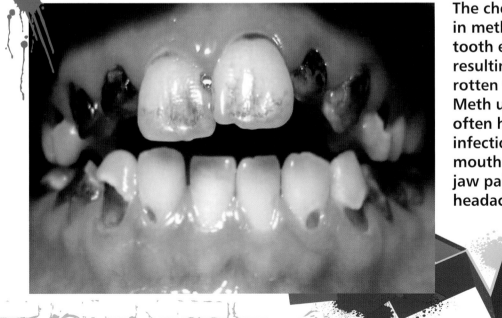

The chemicals in meth erode tooth enamel resulting in rotten teeth. Meth users often have infections, mouth pain, jaw pain, and headaches.

An Impossible Itch

Meth is persuasive stuff. It makes you feel good, but it comes with a very high price tag. During meth hallucinations you may see bugs crawling all over your skin and you itch and pick at them until your skin bleeds and develops sores. These little nasties are called "crank bugs." Even after the meth has worn off, the hallucinations can keep going for days or weeks. This is called prolonged psychosis.

You can expect some pretty shocking physical things to happen to you. You start to look older—fast—and not in a good way. Your eyes sink into your cheeks. You can become freakishly skinny. Sores develop all over your body. Your lips and eyebrows take on a dry, chalky appearance and you sweat heavily. You have a bad odor that no amount of showering can get rid of. Eventually, you develop meth mouth and tooth decay from the lack of saliva in your mouth and because you forget to brush your teeth for days at a time. Not a pretty sight, and not easy to miss.

Meth addicts itch so badly that they pick at their skin, leaving horrible sores and scars.

Chasing the Ghost

After the initial use of crystal meth, the brain sets your pleasure threshold a bit higher than the first time. This means you need a little more crank to get that high you had. The third time, the threshold gets higher again, and you need more meth. And this cycle keeps repeating itself, with the user always needing more meth to get the same high. Users call it "chasing the ghost" or "chasing the dragon."

Meth by Any Other Name

Methamphetamine has many slang names. The names reflects how the drug is used, and what it looks like. The many names shows how quickly it has become commonplace in North American drug culture. Users in different areas may call it different names, but the most common are meth, crystal meth, crystal tina, the poor man's cocaine, the new crack, crank, ice, speed, crystal, go, zoom, glass, redneck, yellow powder, yellow barn, chalk, tick-tock, scootie, and spoosh. Meth that is smoked is called quartz, hot ice, super ice, L.A., L.A. glass, hanyak, batu, and hiropon.

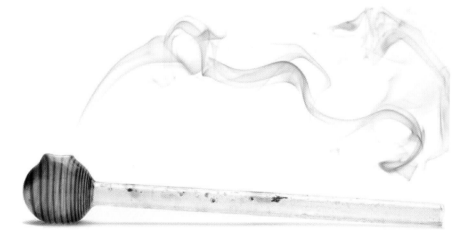

23

Tweaking

Someone who stays on meth for days without coming "down" is said to be tweaking. These tweakers can be dangerous to themselves and others. They are **volatile**, paranoid, and tend to be **psychotic**. The tweaker goes three to 15 days without sleep. At first glance, a tweaker may appear natural, but their eyes are moving faster than

normal, their speech is quick with a slight quiver. If they have mixed the meth with other drugs such as alcohol or marijuana, feelings of paranoia are increased. Tweakers can be very dangerous and should be avoided for safety's sake.

Meth users find resisting the drug very difficult but it can make them feel awful because they may not sleep for days.

Meth Mouth

The key ingredients used to make meth are **corrosive**. When meth is smoked or snorted, these ingredients swirl around the interior of your mouth and rot your teeth. They also burn and irritate the sensitive lining of your mouth causing sores and infection. A mouth full of rotting teeth caused by meth use is often called "meth mouth." Meth users have dry mouths caused by decreased saliva. This allows infection and tooth decay to more easily occur.

Meth users often crave sugar and sugary drinks, which encourages cavities. Cracked teeth are also common as addicts clench their teeth from nervousness and anxiety. Dentists also report that gum disease is more common among meth users because meth decreases the amount of blood flow to the gums causing them to shrink and break down.

Meth users report a strong urge to eat sweets, caused by surging and dropping dopamine levels in the brain. They are often too high to care about brushing their teeth, so tooth decay is also very common.

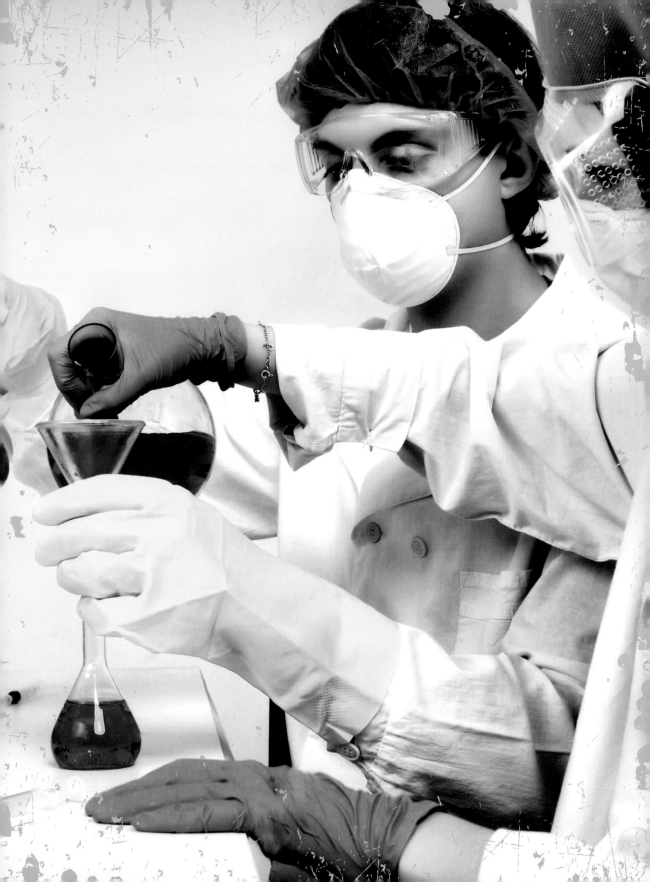

Chapter 4
Meth History

Romanian chemist Lazar Edeleanu developed amphetamines in 1887, while working at a German University. In the 1920s, amphetamines were given a new look and used as medicines for colds, hay fever, and asthma. By 1932, amphetamines were marketed as Benzedrine and used in inhalers for nasal congestion and asthma.

But before that, in 1893, not long after Lazar Edeleanu made amphetamines, a Japanese scientist put a twist on it with a **precursor** chemical called ephedrine and came up with methamphetamine. Methamphetamine was not used for much until World War II. During the war, American, German, Japanese, and English governments started giving it to their troops to make them more efficient soldiers. The drug kept them alert, increased their endurance, and kept them from feeling tired—for a time.

Meth—A Wonder Drug?

In Japan, after the war, factory workers could legally use methamphetamine. It was purchased over the counter and used to keep workers awake during long shifts. Soon, workers became hooked and it was banned in Japan in 1951. In the United States, a prescription was needed for amphetamines. By the 1950s, women were using it as a weight loss pill. Factory workers and students were using amphetamines, including methamphetamine, to stay awake and alert. In 1959, Benzedrine inhalers were banned but amphetamines were still sold to treat many conditions including narcolepsy, hyperactivity, and depression.

In 1965, the Drug Abuse Control Amendments were passed. This law dealt with amphetamines, including methamphetamine, barbiturates and, later, LSD, classifying them as dangerous drugs. This allowed the Food and Drug Administration to recommend that these drugs be controlled. This act was the first time these drugs had been deemed dangerous and prohibited in the United States.

In the 1960s, liquid amphetamine, called "speed," was a well-known drug, often used by "hippies."

Speed Labs

To fill in the gap that this law created, illegal amphetamine, or "speed," labs began springing up across the country. A new type of addict was created—called the "speed freak." Using a liquid form of amphetamine, "speed" was injected directly into a vein. Overdoses resulting in death were common with speed freaks.

Meth Explosion and Solution

Meth continued to be a problem over the years. It was easy to get the ingredients needed to make it—particularly ephedrine and pseudoephedrine used in cold medicines. Meth made big profit for drug gangs who controlled the illegal meth market. In 2005, the Combat Methamphetamine Epidemic Act restricted the sale of ephedrine and pseudoephedrine. Buyers were limited in how much of cold and allergy meds they could purchase at one time. Several states have also enacted laws. In Oregon, cold and allergy meds containing ephedrine and pseudoephedrine can only be obtained with a doctor's prescription. The number of meth labs in the state fell dramatically. Oregon also reported fewer meth-related arrests and fewer users.

Meth Industry

Meth use skyrocket in the 1990s as drug cartels easily purchased massive supplies of ephedrine to make the drug in large "superlabs." Today, most meth is made in small home labs.

Chapter 5
Dependence and Addiction

Addiction is a **compulsive** use of a substance known by the user to be harmful. The problem is not many addicts will admit that their drug of choice is doing them harm. Even when they do, they often can't just quit—it takes more than just willpower to beat a habit like meth. The United Nations has called meth the most abused hard drug in the world.

Meth Addiction

The thing that makes meth appealing is the same thing that makes it so dangerous. Meth jumpstarts the brain's pleasure chemical—dopamine. Users describe the high as so incredible they never want to come down. Meth changes how the brain works and it also destroys the brain's ability to feel pleasure any other way. Over 1.5 million Americans are meth users.

From User to Addict

Meth causes your brain to release a steady stream of dopamine. So much so, that the brain needs to protect itself by reducing the number of receptors sensitive to dopamine. That means the next time you get high, you need more meth. That causes other parts of your brain that control memory, learning, and judgment to physically change. Addiction experts believe meth is one of the hardest addictions to kick because use changes how the brain works.

In a matter of a couple of sessions of meth use, drug-seeking behavior becomes wired into your brain. Drug-seeking behavior means doing everything in search of the next high. It's all you think about, talk about, and plan. It becomes instinctive, like a reflex action.

Signs of Addiction

During your adolescent and teen years, your brain is more susceptible to crystal meth addiction than at any other time of your life. Scientists believe evolution has hard-wired the teen brain to not be averse to risk-taking, so that it is easier for teens to leave the safety of home and go out into the world. However, young brains are still developing and are more likely to become addicted to meth for life. Research shows that users between 12 and 17 years of age could have long-term brain impairment and changed behavior for life.

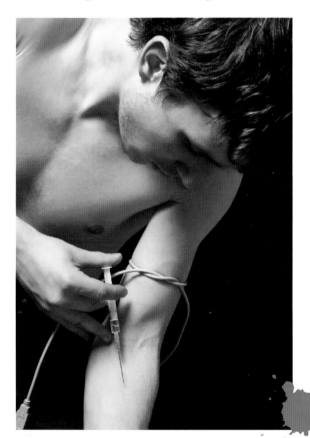

Brain research is a new area of research. Doctors are constantly learning new things about how the brain works when it is addicted to drugs, and how it is permanently changed.

More Risks

Injecting drugs such as meth carries the risk of contracting diseases such as hepatitis C, and HIV, if needles are shared. Many people contract diseases within six months to a year after their first injection.

Needing More

As your behavior changes, you will experience uncontrollable mood swings, aggression, and often violence. Friends and family will notice. It becomes increasingly difficult to hide the rapid weight loss, the drop in grades, and the absences from school. You do weird and bizarre things, such as write a sentence over and over again, or take something apart and put it back together a million times. This is called "punding" and is used to describe behavior in schizophrenics and meth addicts. It's also called "tweaker habits."

Meth use makes it difficult to concentrate on anything other than getting high.

Addicts will do many things to maintain their habit, including stealing from loved ones, or prostituting themselves.

Danger Zone

When your body craves crystal meth, you will do anything to get the drug. You might hang around with people who are criminals, or have unprotected sex with strangers. You may find yourself selling your body for a hit of meth. You use other drugs, such as alcohol and marijuana, to take the edge off the downs and the cravings. You begin needing so much meth just to get high, trying to score becomes a full-time job.

Chapter 6
Seeking Help

Being hooked on crystal meth is a pretty obvious problem, even if you think you have been very good about hiding it. The outward physical signs are a sure-fire giveaway that something is wrong. Even if a friend or a family member has noticed that things are not quite right, reaching out for help can feel terrifying. Sometimes it is forced upon you. For example, the police might call your parents to tell them you're in jail or in the mental health ward of your local hospital.

But what if no one notices you are spiraling out of control? What if everyone looks the other way? What if you really want help but don't know what to do or where to go to find it? Your friends don't care because they get high too. Or maybe you feel you don't have any friends to tell. So what do you do?

A call for help in the middle of the night might be the first step to a life free of crystal meth.

To Tell or Not to Tell?

Choosing to tell someone you have a drug problem can make you feel scared and vulnerable. But the risks of not telling someone you have a meth problem are very serious. Continuing down the path of using methamphetamines can mean losing your family and friends. It's not unusual for your grades to fail, and your physical condition to deteriorate. Meth use leads to serious emotional and physical health issues and possibly death.

Who to Trust?

Meth is very difficult to quit and the idea of quitting often makes users more anxious and suspicious. That makes it even more difficult to voluntarily disclose to someone that you need help. It's okay to feel scared. You may even feel shame. It takes a lot of courage and strength to admit you have a problem. When you ask for help, look for an adult you trust or feel close to, such as a teacher, doctor, friend, or relative. Choose a place where you feel comfortable to have the conversation. If you think you can't say it, write a note or letter. The important thing is to tell someone and be honest about how you feel.

Make a Call

If you can't bring yourself to talk to a person you know, try contacting an organization that knows what you are going through. Many have toll-free numbers to call day or night.

A Friend in Need

What if your friend has the drug problem?
Is there any way you can help?

Listening is a good place to start. It is very difficult to admit you are addicted to a substance, so try not to judge your friend. Encourage them to talk to someone who can help. They might be afraid to talk to someone other than you, so be patient. Let them know they are not alone. When they are ready to make a change, help them find someone they feel they can trust. And don't give up on your friend. Keep listening and encouraging them to get help.

Interventions

It is not uncommon for the drug abuser to be the last person to realize—or accept—that they have a drug problem. Sometimes concerned friends and family decide to have an intervention. Intervening with a meth addict needs to be handled by a professional who is experienced in interventions. An intervention is a delicate situation and emotions run high. Safety is important. A professional counselor must be called in to map out a plan of approach that is safe for all concerned. Addicts are told they have a problem and they need to go to treatment or risk losing the support of loved ones.

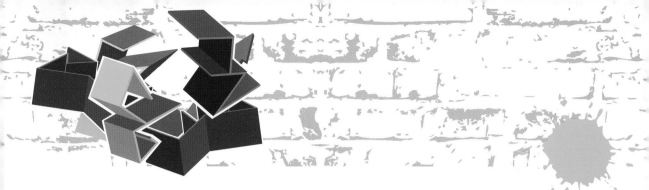

Chapter 7
Treatment and Recovery

Recognizing you have drug problem and telling someone is the first, most important step to recovery. You might even know someone who has gone through treatment and who understands the physical and emotional stages to recovery. Crystal meth is a very addictive drug and quitting is tough.

Triggers and Cravings

The most challenging aspect of treatment and recovery is dealing with the triggers and the cravings for meth. Certain sights, sounds or smells, emotions, being with certain people, or in places that you connect with meth, can "trigger" a release of dopamine into the brain and cause a craving for the drug. Being unable to resist these cravings is psychologically and physically painful. It makes you feel hopeless and powerless. You believe you will never be able to quit and may even relapse. It is important to realize that cravings can be resisted, and that they hold less and less power over you as time goes on.

Withdrawal Symptoms

The severity of the withdrawal symptoms from crystal meth depend on several things, including how long you have been using. The amount of drug routinely used and the duration of use are other factors in withdrawal. **Chronic** users can fight withdrawal symptoms for months.

Withdrawal from any drug is tough. Many users find the symptoms so severe that they are tempted to return to using. Some users will also have to deal with the painful emotions that may have led them to use drugs in the first place. This is why it is important to get help with withdrawal. Trained drug counselors know that addiction isn't just about the drug. They help users deal with their pain in healthier ways.

Withdrawal symptoms include fatigue, anxiety, crazy dreams, pain, and hunger. One of the most serious withdrawal difficulties is feelings of depression. Deprived of dopamine from the drug, users often say they feel empty and joyless. Thoughts of suicide are common. During detox, addicts often feel paranoid and angry. It is important to know these symptoms don't last forever. Although the drug will have changed you, you can regain joy.

Individual Treatment

Treatment can help addicts stop using and recover their lives. Most treatment programs are geared to individual users and their specific issues.

Relapse

Relapse is common, but it doesn't mean failure. Meth addiction is difficult to treat, but not impossible. Drug treatment experts know that relapse may happen once or several times. One key to staying off meth is to change your behavior. This means staying away from people and places that remind you of using crystal meth. This helps minimize the triggers that are associated with the intense cravings. In-patient treatment in a facility where programs and medical help is readily available is the safest road to recovery. These treatment programs help users work on recognizing the patterns that led to abuse. Sometimes, users discover that their addiction has been obscuring a mental health issue. Recovering meth addicts often hit a wall in treatment from one to three months after quitting the drug. They feel their depression deepen as the brain continues to adjust to the drug's absence.

In Treatment

In a treatment program, addicts may be involved in cognitive behavioral intervention. This means they learn to recognize and avoid the situations that led them to do drugs. Sometimes, treatment involves therapy and a focus on other healthy behaviors such as exercise.

Therapy is sometimes more challenging because meth alters the brain and thinking processes. As the brains of young people are still developing, this may mean permanent changes in the way users think and perceive things. All of this is workable. Addiction has a life-long recovery process, particularly for meth addicts.

Recovering addicts learn to deal with their challenges and adapt to new realities. Treatment experts encourage recovering meth addicts to realize that they can live successfully and happily without the drug.

Meth recovery requires special treatment and aftercare. Recovering addicts need to learn how to live life without meth.

How to Cope

Support groups help recovering addicts talk through their experiences. Sharing your fears helps you feel less alone. You will probably be scared and doubt your ability to stay clean. That's to be expected. Keeping a journal of your progress will help you see how far you have come. It is normal to feel depressed, frustrated, and alone. Your circle of friends will change, especially if they are still using meth. Talk to a social worker or call a hotline. Check out what options are available in your community. There may be alternative therapies available such as acupuncture, massage, meditation, and exercises to help with the restlessness and changes you are experiencing. Recovery takes time. Ask for support, talk it out, and give yourself time to get well and heal.

Resources

There is plenty of frightening information on the Internet about meth use and its consequences. Not all of these sites are vetted for accurate, unbiased information. Look for websites that offer support that is non-judgmental or isn't tied to one specific rehab method or service. Visit your library for books that contain factual information. Libraries are information storehouses that can also assist you in locating organizations that provide assistance to drug users in need of help. Here are some trustworthy resources to start with:

Books

Tweak: Growing Up on Methamphetamines, by Nic Sheff (Simon & Schuster Children's Publishing, 2009)

Beautiful Boy: A Father's Journey Through His Son's Addiction, by David Sheff (Houghton Miffin Harcourt, 2008)

Websites

Above the Influence
www.abovetheinfluence.com
This is an online resource that provides information about drug abuse, as well as information about resources that you can access. This website is written for teens and provides information to help make decisions about abusing drugs, addiction, and recovery.

www.teens.drugabuse.gov
This site for teens and adolescents offers information on crystal meth and other drugs. The site offers blogs, downloads, and information for parents and teachers.

www.findtreatment.samhsa.gov
Or call 1–800–662–HELP
This is a government site that helps you locate treatment programs and facilities all over the United States.

www.montanameth.org
The Montana Meth Project website is aimed specifically at teens with meth abuse issues. Its purpose is to educate and inform users and potential users of the risks involved with crystal meth. It's hard-hitting and does not pull punches.

Organizations, Hotlines, and Helplines
Substance Abuse and Mental Health Service Administration (SAMHSA) (1-800-662-HELP)
(www.samhsa.gov)
This agency has a hotline and website and can help you locate treatment centers, help agencies, and counselors in your area. Their hotline operates 24 hours a day, 7 days a week and is staffed by compassionate and knowledgeable professionals who can help you take the first step in getting help.

Narcotics Anonymous
(www.na.org)
This website will give you information about the support systems that are available in your community.

Glossary

adage A short statement that expresses a truth

agitated Nervous or disturbed

blood pressure The pressure of the blood in the body's circulatory system; it is closely related to the force and rate of the heartbeat

chronic Something that is persistant or difficult to change

compulsive An irresistible urge that often goes against a person's wishes

corrosive Damaging

dehydration A process during which a person loses a large amount of water

enamel The hard, glossy substance that covers a tooth

euphoric Feeling intensely happy or excited

hallucinations An experience where a person perceives, or feels something that is not real or present

hemorrhage When blood escapes from a damaged or ruptured blood vessel

libido Sexual desire

MRI scans Magnetic Resonance Imaging scan of the body that produces images of the internal organs

narcolepsy A medical condition that causes a person to fall asleep at inappropriate times

nervous system The nerve tissues that control the activities of the body, brain, and spinal cord; also called the central nervous system

paranoia A mental condition in which a person loses touch with reality; it includes extreme fear or delusions, and a mistrust of people and their actions without reason or evidence for justification

pharmaceutical Relating to medicines or medicinal drugs

precursor Something that comes before another thing

psychotic A person who suffers from psychosis, a mental disorder in which thoughts and emotions are impaired and reality is lost

relapse A return to a habit or drug use after stopping

tolerance When someone has been using a drug for a long time and the drug's effects have lessened, requiring larger doses to maintain the desired effect

volatile Something or someone that is liable to change rapidly or unpredictably, and often violently

Index